HOW BIG IS IT?

A BIG Book All About BIGness

by Ben Hillman

SCHOLASTIC REFERENCE
An Imprint of
SCHOLASTIC
www.scholastic.com

Library of Congress Cataloging-in-Publication Data
Hillman, Ben 1957-
How big is it? : a big book all about bigness / by Ben
Hillman.
p. cm.
1. Size perception—Juvenile literature. 2. Size
judgment—Juvenile literature. I. Title.

BF299.S5H55 2007
153.7'52—dc22

ISBN-13: 978-0-439-91808-4
ISBN-10: 0-439-91808-1

10 9 8 7 6 5 4 3 2 1   07 08 09 10 11/0

Printed in Singapore

First printing, September 2007

Cover design by Red Herring Design

CONTENTS

55.2 feet
(16.8 m)

Giant Squid
Architeuthis dux

Presenting one of the great Mysteries of the Deep! For decades, people searched for the Giant Squid. The only ones ever seen were dead or dying creatures floating near the surface. The Giant Squid had *never* been seen alive in its natural habitat deep in the sea. Scientists tried everything from putting cameras on deep-sea submersibles to attaching cameras to sperm whales! But no luck. All we knew about this mysterious creature is how big it gets: *really* big.

The biggest one ever found washed ashore in Lyall Bay, New Zealand, in 1887. It measured an astonishing 55 feet, 2 inches, in length (16.8 m).

The Giant Squid also has the largest eyes in the entire animal kingdom, reaching over 18 inches in diameter (0.46 m) — the size of your typical beach ball.

Finally, in 2004, some Japanese scientists went searching deep in the North Pacific Ocean using baited fishing lines to attract the elusive monster — and caught one on film!

It was a smallish giant, only about 26 feet (8 m) in length, but they watched in fascination as the creature grappled for the bait in a "ball of tentacles." Shining their lights through the pitch darkness at 2,950 feet (900 m) under the sea (over half a mile!), they watched the colossal struggle. Finally the squid broke free, losing an 18-foot-long tentacle (5.5 m) in the bargain.

Want to know more about the fabled Giant Squid? Get in a submarine, bring a giant tub of calamari sauce, and go find one!

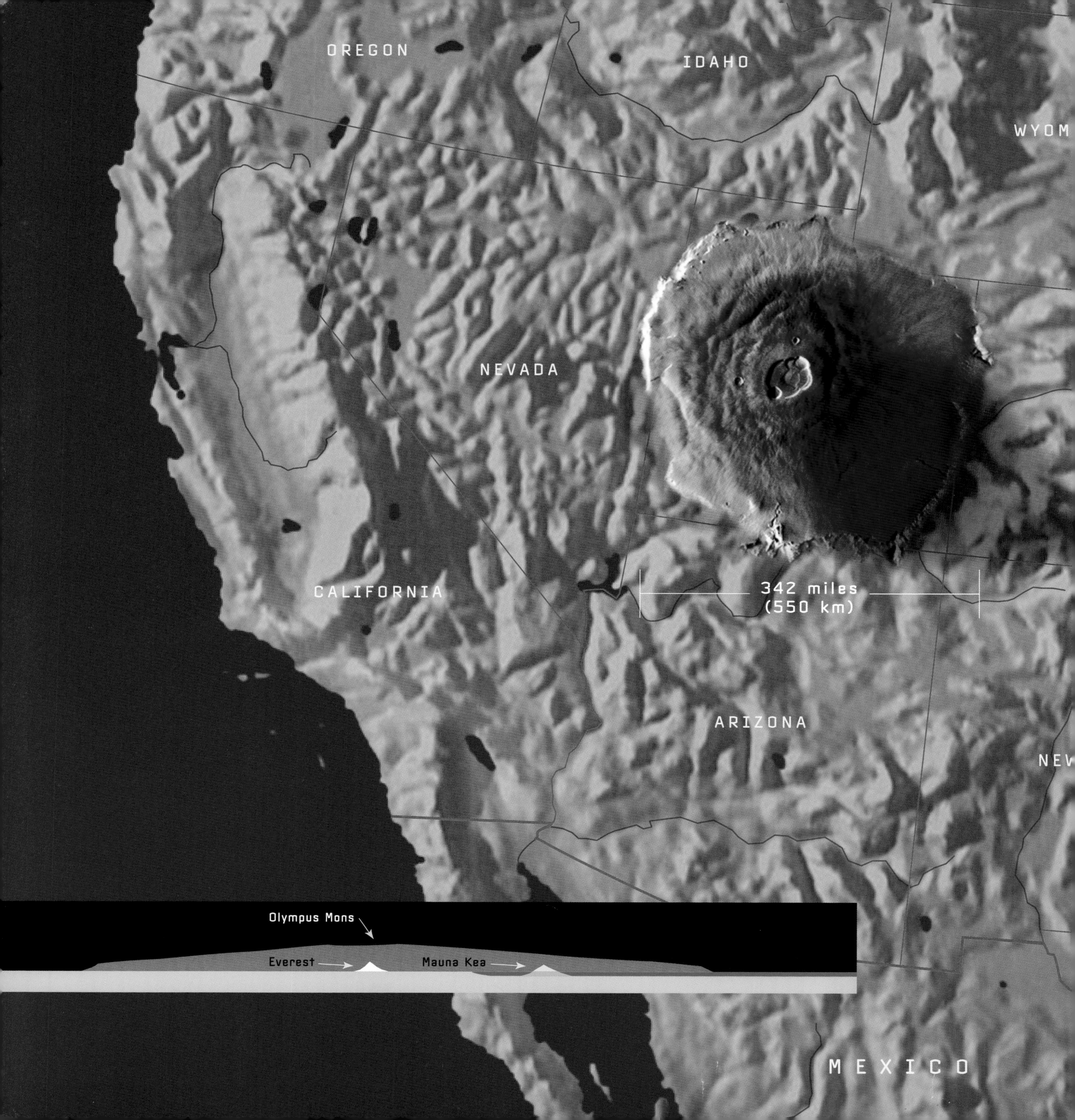

OREGON

IDAHO

WYOM

NEVADA

342 miles
(550 km)

CALIFORNIA

ARIZONA

NEW

Olympus Mons

Everest   Mauna Kea

MEXICO

SOUTH DAKOTA

NEBRASKA

COLORADO

KANSAS

Olympus Mons

CO

MARS

Olympus Mons

The largest mountain in the solar system is on Mars. The mighty volcano Olympus Mons measures 342 miles across (550 km) — about the same size as Utah! It reaches 15 miles (24 km) above the surface of Mars. At the top is a volcanic crater 56 miles (90 km) across and two miles deep (3.2 km). At the outer edges of the mountain are cliffs four miles high (6.4 km). Big enough for you?

Mars is so small (about half the size of Earth), and Olympus Mons is so large, that when you look at the whole planet, Olympus Mons looks like a giant wart.

How long did it take to grow that big? It started erupting around 3.8 billion years ago and lava was flowing down its sides as recently as two million years ago. It may *still* be an active volcano, ready to blow.

Back on Earth, our puny Mount Everest stands about 5.5 miles high (8.9 km), but Everest is much harder to climb. The ascent up Olympus Mons would be more like a pleasant stroll than a climb. It's shaped like a giant pancake with a slope so gentle you would hardly notice it. So if you go, don't take any fancy mountain-climbing gear. Just a regular old space suit.

And speaking of the tallest mountain on Earth, did you know that it's not Mount Everest at all? It's Mauna Kea in Hawaii. The only problem is that poor Mauna Kea starts 19,684 feet (6,000 m) below the ocean so it doesn't reach as high in the sky as Everest. But it peaks out at a whopping six miles (9.66 km) from base to top — almost a mile taller than Everest.

Length: 33 feet
(10 m)

Reticulated Python
Python reticulatus

The reticulated python is the longest snake in the world. The largest one ever found was spotted on the island of Sulawesi in Indonesia. Stretched out, it measured a humongous 33 feet (10 m) in length. Much too long to stretch out on your sofa and munch on a snack of wild pig. Although it's the world record-holder in length, the "retic" is relatively slim compared to its famous rival, the anaconda, which is considered not the longest, but the *biggest* snake in the world because of its impressive girth.

In case you're wondering just what in the world "reticulated" means, it refers to the pattern on the python's back — a network of patterns and colors that is unique to this species. Usually this pattern consists of diamond shapes running along its back bordered with black and yellow.

Reticulated pythons live in the tropical forests of southeast Asia. They can be found all the way from Malaysia to Borneo, Java, Sumatra, and the Philippines. You can find them slithering on the ground, curled up in caves, or hanging out in trees. They have even settled happily in some large cities in that part of the world. But keep your distance, because these giant reptiles get very hungry. What's for dinner? Monkeys, wild boar, antelope, and sometimes even people.

Some people think that pythons make good pets. They don't play fetch and you might not want to curl up in bed with one, but take your snake for a walk and you'll probably have the sidewalk all to yourself.

40 feet
(12.2 m)

Quetzalcoatlus
Quetzalcoatlus northropi

Look! Up in the sky! It's a bird! It's a plane! Nope, it's the flying reptile *Quetzalcoatlus northropi* — the largest creature that ever flew!

With a wingspan of almost 40 feet across (12.2 m), the Quetzalcoatlus spans a width the same as an F-18 Hornet fighter jet.

Fossils of other ancient flying reptiles like pterodactyls were discovered a few hundred years ago. They measured a measly 25 feet (7.6 m) across.

Then in 1971, a student at the University of Texas named Doug Lawson discovered the first bones of this 40-foot creature in Big Bend National Park. Doug named it Quetzalcoatlus after the Aztec feathered serpent god.

And what a beast it was. It had giant bat-like wings made of skin that stretched from its body to an *extremely* long pinky finger that extended from its claws to the tip of the wing — over 12 feet (3.7 m) in length. It had long, slender, toothless jaws and, unlike other flying reptiles, no tail at all.

But could the Quetzalcoatlus really fly? Paleontologists and aeronautical engineers have studied the bones and tried to figure out what this reptile could actually do. They're still arguing about it. Some say it could fly. Some say that it couldn't fly at all, but only glide. Maybe it jumped off of cliffs to begin its flight? Whatever the answer, its giant wings would have allowed it to soar for great distances through the strange Mesozoic skies.

You wouldn't want to get hit by those droppings!

449 feet
(137 m)

Great Pyramid at Giza

Ladies and gentlemen, presenting one of the Seven Wonders of the Ancient World! The Grandest Gravestone Ever Gazed Upon by Gasping Globe-trotters! The Great Pyramid of Cheops! Or Khufu! Or however you say it.

For 40 centuries, this pyramid was the tallest structure in the entire world. Built by the Egyptian Pharaoh Khufu (or Cheops) around 2560 B.C., the Great Pyramid stood at 481 feet high (147 m). Now, having lost a bit off the top, it's 449 feet high (137 m). If you could go to Giza by subway, it would take eight subway cars chugging up the side to reach the pyramid's peak.

Building this pyramid was one of the largest employment projects in the ancient world. It was made by piling up 2,300,000 stone blocks — each weighing an average of two and a half tons (2,268 kg). That scales out to about 6.5 million tons of rock (5,900 kg). The whole base of the pyramid covers 13 acres.

As you can imagine, using human power alone, it took a while to construct. A recent calculated guess is that it took five thousand people about 20 years to build, not including coffee breaks.

Now why did Mr. Cheops (or Khufu) want to build such a thing? As a monument to himself, naturally. When he died, his sarcophagus was placed in a chamber in the heart of the pyramid where he could begin his mysterious journey into the afterlife.

Did the Pharaoh's mysterious journey to the afterlife begin on the Q train? We'll probably never know.

12 inches
(30 cm)

Goliath Bird-eating Spider
Theraphosa blondi

Little Miss Muffet sat on a tuffet, eating her curds and whey. Along came a spider, who sat down beside her, and scared the living daylights out of her because this was a *Theraphosa blondi*, the biggest spider on Earth!

Measuring a disgusting 10–12 inches across (25–30 cm), this hairy beast is the size of a dinner plate. It can be found in the rain forests of South America, living in burrows built in soggy swamps.

And yes, it has been known to eat small birds — which it drags from their nests in a flurry of hairy grasping legs and piercing venomous fangs. The poor bird has tweeted its last tweet. Then the Goliath carries its victim down into its burrow for dinner.

Not having a set of silverware or even teeth for that matter, the Goliath has its own revolting way of devouring its prey. It spits digestive juices onto its meal. The juices eat away at the soft parts of the body, reducing it to soup that the Goliath then slurps up with gusto.

The Goliath also eats frogs, snakes, beetles, lizards, bats, and baby rats. But thankfully not people. If you're unlucky enough to get bitten, the venom may sting a bit for a few hours, but it won't kill you.

And even more reassuring, you can be warned ahead of time by actually *hearing* these spiders. Unlike the typical silent spider, the Goliath bird-eater can make a loud hissing noise by rubbing the bristles on its legs together. Run!

1,720 feet
(524 m)

Tsunami

The greatest surfing survival story of all time happened on July 9, 1958, in peaceful Lituya Bay, Alaska.

Anchored in the narrow bay surrounded by snowcapped peaks, a father and son watched the sunset from their fishing boat, the *Edrie,* when a massive earthquake struck. They heard a deafening boom as the entire wall of mountains at the far end of the bay collapsed. About 40 million cubic yards of rock and glacier slammed into the bay — *mega splash!*

On the *Edrie*, the father and son watched in horror as the wall of water approached them. The wave shot up and rocketed across the bay, reaching as high as 1,720 feet (524 m) as it roared up the mountainsides, wiping out everything in its path, killing millions of trees and stripping away the earth right down to naked bedrock.

But miraculously, their little boat was lifted up by the onrushing torrent. The *Edrie* rode the giant wave out to sea and got tossed back into the bay in the backwash, leaving the two witnesses amazed at their good luck.

Could a wave like that hit a big city like Tokyo? This picture shows what it might look like if a Lituya-size wave hit.

The Lituya wave was unique because of the narrow shape of Lituya Bay and the surrounding wall of mountains. Tokyo gets rocked repeatedly by earthquakes, but it lies on flat terrain, so a giant wave is less likely.

But you never know, so don't leave your surfboard at home.

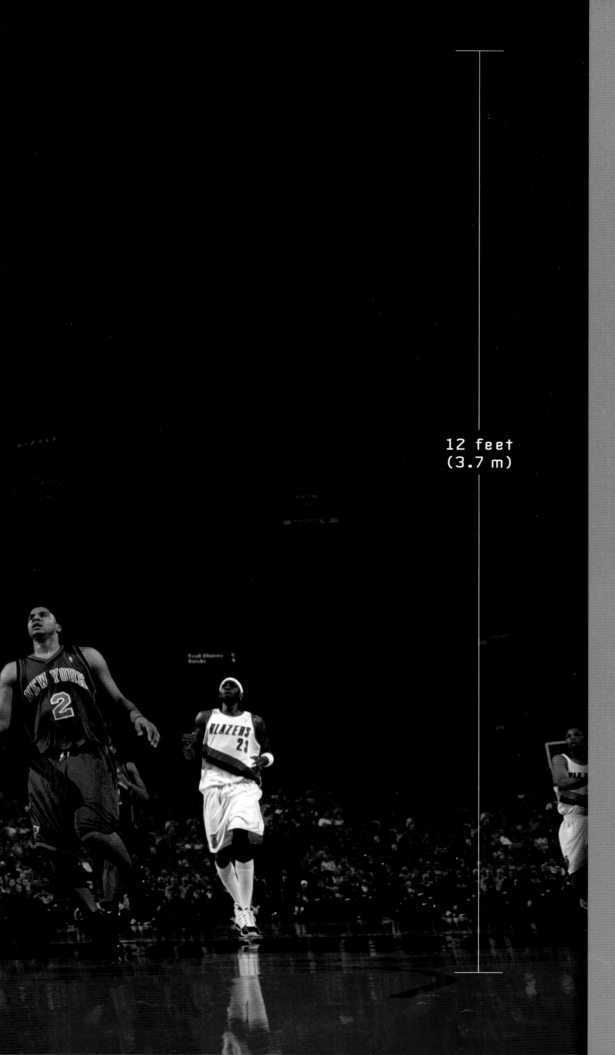

**12 feet
(3.7 m)**

Polar Bear

Slam dunks are no problem for this guy.

Polar bears are the largest carnivores on Earth. And when they stand on their hind legs, they're the tallest. The biggest polar bear anyone ever saw stood an astounding 12 feet tall (3.7 m). That's two feet higher than the rim of a basketball net.

Kodiak bears (also called Alaskan brown bears) and polar bears are the biggest bears known, but standing up, the polar bear is definitely champion. Tigers, the next biggest carnivore, are only half as big.

Polar bears live in the far north, all the way around the Arctic Circle, from northern Canada to Greenland to Norway and across Russia — wherever there is ice and a nice menu of seals. When chasing down a seal or charging down a basketball court, their speed is formidable. For short distances, a polar bear can charge along at 25 miles per hour (40 km/h) — almost as fast as the fastest Olympic sprinter.

Male polar bears are the biggest. They can grow two to three times the size of females. The largest male polar bear ever recorded weighed 2,209 pounds (1,002 kg) — over a ton!

Another amazing thing about polar bears is their sense of smell. A polar bear can sniff out a seal 20 miles (32 km) away.

By the way, they can also sniff out *you*. Polar bears are one of the few animals that will hunt humans for food. So if you do have a polar bear on your basketball team, by the time the game is over, you might end up with fewer players than you started with.

27 inches
(70 cm)

Dragonfly of the Carboniferous
Meganeura monyi

Three hundred million years ago, before dinosaurs ruled the earth, was a time called the Carboniferous Period. The planet was much warmer then. It was wet and swampy with fantastically lush vegetation.

And there was over 70% more oxygen in the air than there is today, making most living things much bigger than their modern-day counterparts. It was like all of life was in overdrive.

Giant ferns as tall as trees stretched high into the sky. Ancient relatives of millipedes grew to six feet long (1.8 m) — also called "godzillapedes." Ferocious two-foot-long scorpions scuttled over the ground.

And insects were enormous.

Because the size of an insect is limited by the amount of oxygen that can get into its body, more oxygen meant bigger bugs. And some of them, for the first time in history, took to the air.

The biggest insect was the dragonfly. They grew to the size of hawks and swooped through the skies — the largest flying insects that ever lived. Modern dragonflies have been clocked at over 30 miles per hour (48 km/h). Bigger dragonflies usually fly faster than smaller ones. Who knows how fast *Meganeura monyi* could zip through the oxygenated atmosphere?

One thing is for sure: if one of these wiped out on your windshield, you'd know it.

2 miles
(3.2 km)

Ice Age Glacier

We were practically an ice planet.

As late as ten thousand years ago, there were sheets of ice up to two miles thick (3.2 km) that covered most of the northern hemisphere. As the world got colder, these sheets traveled south from the Arctic regions. Trillions of tons of ice leveled the landscape and bulldozed mountain-size piles of soil and rock over a thousand miles (1,609 km). So much water was locked up in the ice sheets that the sea level fell by 410 feet (125 m).

If you glance to your left, you'll see what it would look like if a two-mile-high glacier crept up on Chicago. If you live there, you'd end up being a Popsicle. Fortunately the North American ice sheet won't make its next appearance for a few more millennia.

Major ice ages can last anywhere from 30 to 200 million years. During these ice ages, glaciers advance and retreat fairly often. Actually, we are still considered to be in an ice age today. This is just a short warm period during a glacial retreat.

But you can still see huge boulders that were left over when the ice sheets last retreated thousands of years ago. If you happen to spot a really big rock just sitting in an open field, it could be one of these "glacial erratics."

Glaciers nowadays are retreating faster than ever, which leads most scientists to believe that it is a sign of global warming due to human activity — like pollution from carbon dioxide emissions. But not to worry. All we have to do is wait ten thousand years and we can cool off in the next ice age.

805 feet
(245 m)

232 feet
(71 m)

21 feet
(6 m)

Airship

Imagine an ocean liner floating through the air. That was the size of the German airship *Hindenburg* — the biggest thing that ever took to the skies. At 804 feet (245 m), it was more than three times longer than a Boeing 747 and 38 times longer than the Wright Brothers' first airplane.

There are two kinds of airships: blimps and zeppelins. The *Hindenburg* was a zeppelin — a rigid airship with an internal metal frame. A blimp has no structural framework and is more like a big balloon. (Today's blimps are about one quarter of the size of the *Hindenburg*.)

Built in Germany in 1936, the mighty *Hindenburg* made many successful voyages across the Atlantic, usually arriving in the U.S. in Lakehurst, New Jersey, and sometimes in Brazil. Although gigantic in size, the *Hindenburg* could hold only 70 passengers, as opposed to a Boeing 747 jetliner, which holds up to 524.

But travel was different on a zeppelin. The average transatlantic voyage took over two days. The *Hindenburg* passengers each had small sleeping quarters and could spend their time strolling about the promenade deck looking at spectacular views of the earth 1,000 feet (305 m) below as they cruised at a leisurely 78 miles per hour (126 km/h).

One problem: the *Hindenburg* was filled with seven million cubic feet (198,000 m³) of highly flammable hydrogen gas. On May 6, 1937, the *Hindenburg* exploded in a fiery disaster while trying to land in New Jersey, ending the era of the great zeppelins forever.

(10 km)

Dinosaur-killing Asteroid

Actually it hit in Mexico. But this is how big it was compared to New York City.

Sixty-five million years ago, an asteroid about six miles (10 km) across slammed into the earth at around 45,000 miles per hour (73,000 km/h), penetrating and melting the earth's crust, sending a plume of magma into the stratosphere, creating massive tsunamis, setting huge fires all over the planet, rocketing millions of tons of debris into the atmosphere, covering the planet in a cloud of soot that plunged the world into darkness for months, plummeting the temperature, freezing the globe into one endless winter night, and sending the dinosaurs to extinction.

How do we know this? From the element iridium. Iridium is rare on Earth but is common in asteroids. In 1980, the physicists Luis and Walter Alvarez were examining a thin rock layer that was formed on Earth just at the time that the dinosaurs went extinct. They found the rock had twenty-five times more iridium than normal.

That pointed to one conclusion: a giant asteroid must have hit the earth and its iridium dust drifted around the planet.

Soon evidence for the crater was discovered. At the tip of Mexico's Yucatán Peninsula, geologists found telltale signs that there used to be a crater at least 110 miles wide (180 km) that was formed just around the time of the mass extinction.

The evidence is almost certain. What killed the dinosaurs came from outer space.

13 inches
(33 cm)
ACTUAL SIZE

Egg of the Elephant Bird
Aepyornis maximus

Once upon a time in the land of Madagascar, there lived the biggest bird that ever was. It stood ten feet high. (The lowly ostrich only stands eight feet high.)

It stomped around for roughly a million years or so before going extinct in the 1600s. (The arrival of humans on Madagascar 2,000 years ago may have had something to do with this. Think omelets.)

Some people think the elephant bird was the basis for the legend of the giant bird called the roc from the tales of Sinbad. But we know the elephant bird was real because it left behind some bones and a huge number of eggshells. And when mommy elephant bird laid an egg, it was a whopper.

In fact, this is not only the biggest bird egg, but the biggest any-kind-of-egg. Bigger than the biggest dinosaur egg.

The biggest elephant bird egg ever found was 13 inches (33 cm) across and weighed over 20 pounds (9 kg). It held over 2 gallons (9 l) of liquid, including yolk and egg white. That's as big as 8 ostrich eggs. Or 180 chicken eggs. Or 12,000 hummingbird eggs.

Speaking of hummingbirds, the little guy sitting atop the elephantine elephant bird egg is the bee hummingbird of Cuba — the smallest bird in the world. In Cuba it is called the *zunzún*. It's about two and a half inches long (~6.4 cm) and weighs four *thousandths* of a pound (1.8 g) — lighter than a U.S. penny. And the egg of the bee hummingbird is, naturally, the smallest egg in the world. About the size of a pea.

378.1 feet
(115.2 m)

Redwood
Sequoia sempervirens

Where is the tallest tree in the world? Actually, it's a secret. But we'll give you a clue. It's not in Brooklyn, New York, as shown here. It happens to be growing somewhere in Redwood National Park near Eureka, California. But the rangers won't tell you exactly which tree it is.

Why? Because the last time they pointed out the world's tallest tree, so many people went to see it that they trampled the ground and the top of the tree died and fell off. No more tallest tree.

The current Tallest Tree in the World has the name Hyperion. It is a thousand-year-old coast redwood standing at 378.1 feet (115.2 m). But even at that amazing height, it doesn't stand out in a crowd. It's in a grove of redwoods, all of which are giants, so it's not obvious which one is actually the tallest.

Hyperion is the *current* tallest tree in the world, but it's nowhere near the tallest tree known in history. That award belongs to an Australian eucalyptus, at Watts River, Victoria, that was alive in the 1800s. That tree is believed, with a great degree of certainty, to have stood at over 492 feet (150 m). That's about as tall as Mount Rushmore.

By the way, *tallest* does not mean *biggest*. Biggest means mass, not just height. We used to think that the General Sherman giant sequoia was the biggest living thing on Earth. But that honor now belongs to a 2,200-acre (890 hectare) giant fungus that's living underground in Oregon State. That one is probably *not* a tourist attraction.

564 feet
(172 m)

Akula (Shark) Submarine

This leviathan of the deep is one of the most dangerous machines imaginable — a giant submersible weapon of mass destruction. The Russians call it an Akula (Shark) class submarine. In the western world, it is nicknamed Typhoon.

It is the largest submarine in the world.

It measures 564 feet (172 m) in length. If an Akula sub happened to surface in the middle of Turner Field in Atlanta — with its nose pointed at home plate — its tail would be sitting 163 feet (50 m) beyond the center field fence. This could disrupt the game and annoy the spectators.

Back in the 1980s, the Akula was armed with 20 intercontinental ballistic missiles, and each missile with ten nuclear warheads, and all were aimed at the United States. And America's giant Ohio class submarines had missiles aimed at Russia. (The Ohio subs are three feet [1 m] shorter, so the Russians still claim the record for Biggest Sub.)

Now the United States and Russia are more friendly and only one of the Akula class subs is still roaming the seas. And it can roam quite far. The Akula is powered by a nuclear reactor and can disappear underwater for four months at a time without refueling. It can dive down to 1,640 feet (500 m).

But for all its size and strength, the Akula hardly makes a whisper. Silence is golden in the submarine world and, surprisingly, bigger submarines can run far more silently than smaller ones do.

P. S. Playing center field in this park must be a bummer.

18 feet
(5.5 m)

Giraffe
Giraffa camelopardalis

Meet our gentlest giant — the giraffe. The giraffe is the tallest of all living animals. The males can grow up to 18 feet tall (5.5 m) — that's almost as tall as a two-story house.

So if you do insist on keeping a giraffe, make sure you get permission to saw through the ceiling so that he can live comfortably.

Being the tallest animal on the plains of Africa does a lot for a giraffe. First of all, it allows it to see predators coming from a great distance. Although a grown giraffe doesn't usually get attacked by predators like lions and leopards, their calves do. As soon as a grown-up giraffe spots a predator, it bellows a warning to the rest of the herd and they all gallop away with their graceful long-legged gait at up to 35 miles per hour (56 km/h).

Being the tallest animal allows the giraffe to happily munch away on leaves that no one else can reach. Their favorite meal is the thorny acacia leaf, which they grab with their dexterous 1.5-foot-long (46 cm) blue-black tongues. Somehow they know how to reach around the thorns without getting poked.

But being so tall also has its disadvantages. When a giraffe bends down to drink at a water hole, it spreads its legs out in such an awkward position that it makes it difficult for the giraffe to stand back up quickly. That's why there's always one giraffe keeping watch for predators while others are drinking.

By the way, a giraffe has seven vertebrae in its neck — just like you. But in a giraffe, each bone is over ten inches long!

35

1,000 feet
(305 m)

Arecibo Radio Telescope

Come in, Andromeda! The Arecibo radio telescope is the largest single-dish telescope in the world. Set into a natural bowl-shaped valley in the hills of northwest Puerto Rico, the telescope measures a whopping 1,000 feet (305 m) across — almost as wide as the Eiffel Tower is tall. That's a dish that could hold maybe half a billion bowls of breakfast cereal!

But this isn't the type of telescope you look through with an eyepiece. This is a radio telescope — collecting radio waves streaming in from outer space. Not that we hear pop music from the Andromeda galaxy, although we'd like to. These are naturally occurring cosmic radio waves.

Some of these waves come from a great distance — millions of light years. By the time they arrive here, they're *very* weak. So if you've got a radio telescope, bigger is better.

Astronomers don't actually *listen* to these radio waves. They make pictures with the waves — the same way we make photographs out of light — to find out all sorts of things.

Arecibo has proven its worth. Using it, astronomers determined the rotation rate of Mercury, found the first planet orbiting another star, took the first picture of an asteroid, and found the first binary pulsar (two ultra-dense radio-emitting stars orbiting each other) — this won a Nobel Prize!

Arecibo is also the hero of the famous SETI@home project. Home computers all over the world join up to sift through Arecibo data, looking for signals from intelligent life from outer space. You never know who might be trying to contact *you*!

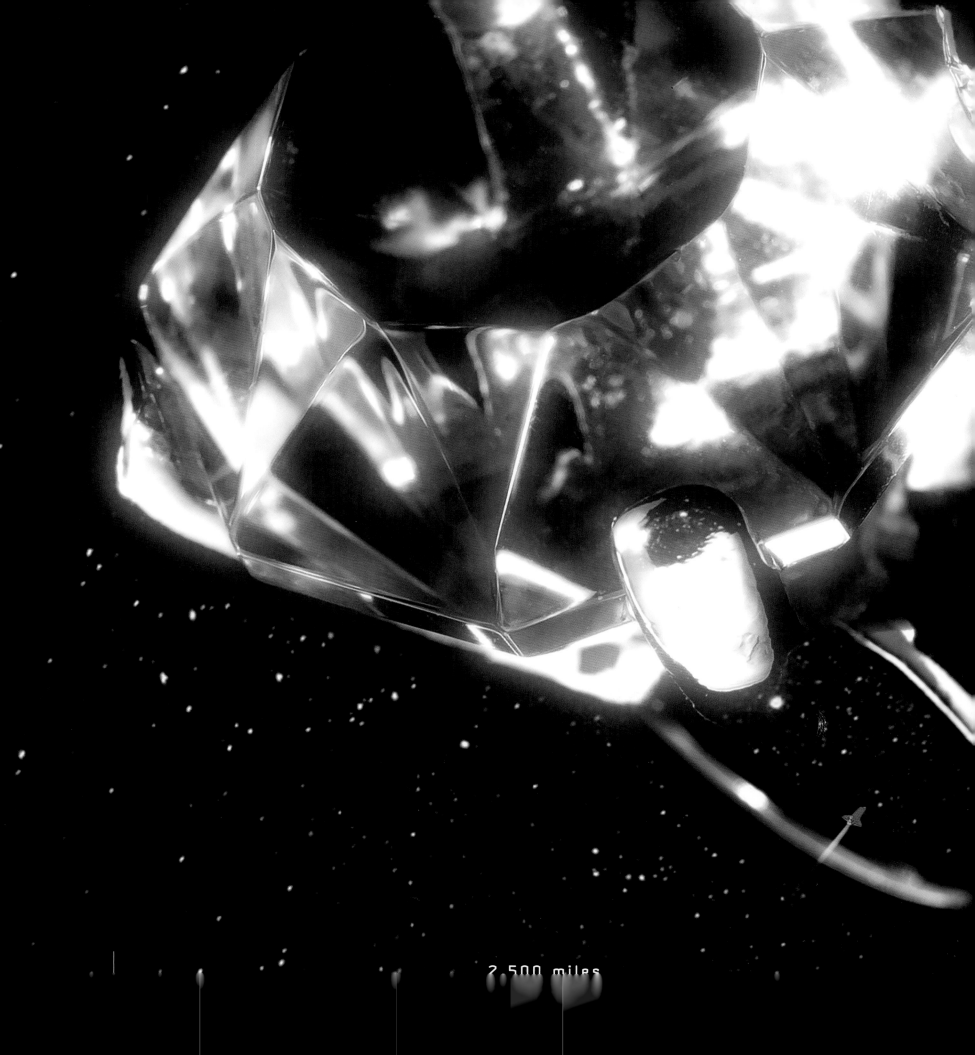

2,500 miles

Diamond

Up above the world so high,
Like a ridiculously enormous
diamond in the sky...

OK, OK, it doesn't really look like this! Actually, the biggest diamond in the world isn't in the world; it's in outer space. And it doesn't look like a giant engagement ring.

What is it? It's the core of a white dwarf star in the constellation Centaurus — a humongous piece of crystallized carbon that is approximately 2,500 miles (~4,000 km) across. They figure it weighs in at about 10 billion trillion trillion carats. The biggest diamond on earth is the Star of Africa, which weighs a paltry 530 carats.

Astronomers named the diamond-centered star Lucy, after the Beatles' song "Lucy in the Sky with Diamonds."

So how in the world do they know that in the middle of teeny tiny dim little Lucy 50 light-years away is the Mother of all Diamonds? Well, first it was a theory.

When stars the size of the sun (or smaller) get old (10 billion years old or so), they run out of fuel and collapse into white dwarf stars. The center of these stars is carbon, and astronomers figured that the intense pressure from the star falling in on itself compresses the carbon into diamond.

Scientists were able to confirm this by studying the pulsing light that comes out of Lucy. They can tell what's going on in the middle of the star, the same way that they can study seismic waves and tell what's going on in the middle of the earth.

Brace yourself! It's a diamondquake!

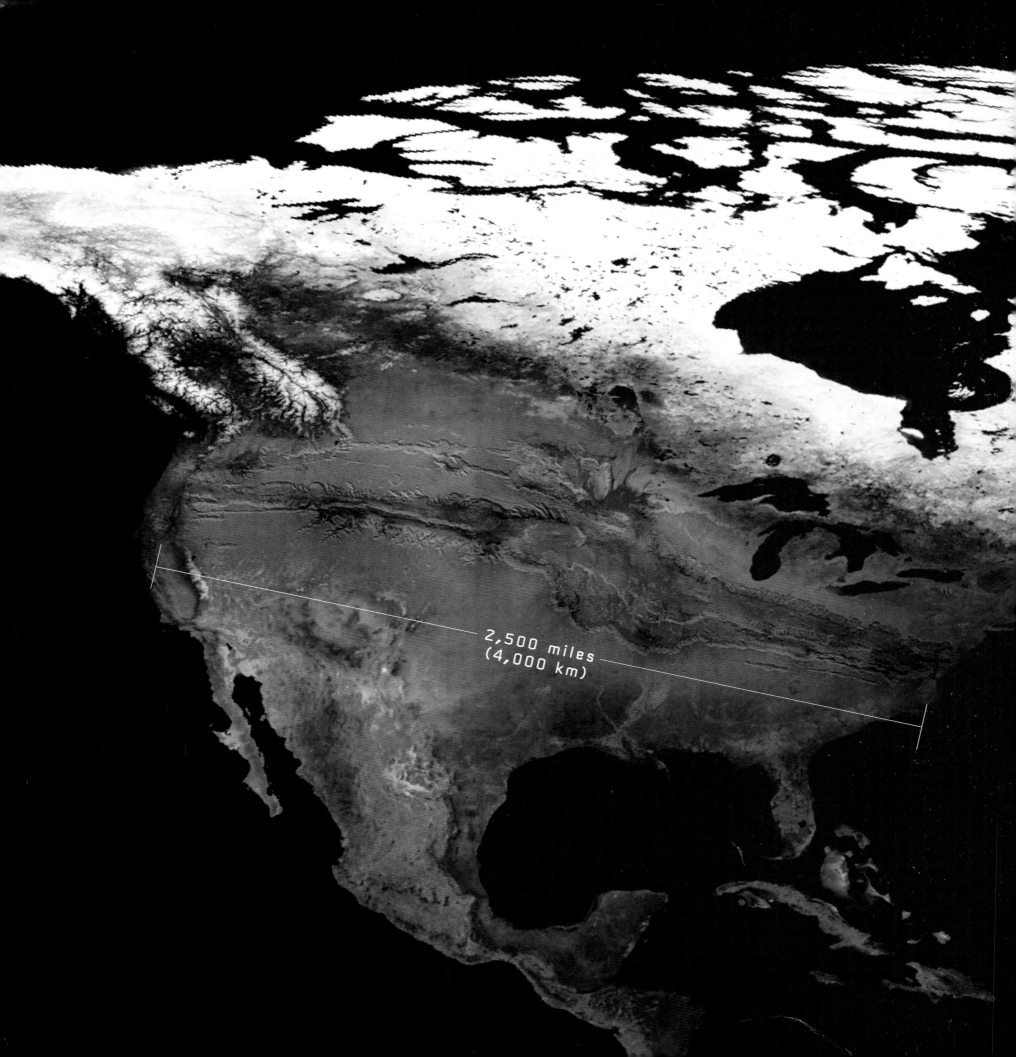

2,500 miles
(4,000 km)

Valles Marineris

Valles Marineris

The Grand Canyon just can't compare to the great crack in the side of Mars called Valles Marineris.

This is the biggest known canyon in the solar system. It's a crevice as long as the entire United States. On Mars, which is much smaller than Earth, Valles Marineris stretches almost a fifth of the way around the whole planet.

It's so deep that if you bungee-jumped off the side, you'd be jumping at the same height as if you had stepped out of a jet airliner in mid-flight. Six miles (10 km) straight down and you'd hit the bottom.

The canyon probably formed billions of years ago as the Martian crust cooled. The tectonic plates solidified and cracked apart — just like a cake might when you take it out of the oven.

Valles Marineris was first discovered in 1971 by the spacecraft *Mariner 9*. That's where the canyon got its name. Until then, the surface of Mars was a complete mystery. Now satellites are mapping the whole planet in extraordinary detail.

Some of the ancient channels running out of the canyon were probably formed by running water. The history of water on Mars is still being studied. Clearly Mars was wet in its past, but how much water there was and how recently it disappeared are still questions under investigation. Some people think there might *still* be water on Mars — maybe just below the surface.

Watch for thirsty Little Green Men.

3 feet
(91 cm)

Flower
Rafflesia arnoldii

In 1818, Sir Stamford Raffles, Governor of Sumatra, and his friend, Dr. Joseph Arnold, were riding on horseback through the diabolically dense jungle near Bengkulu, when suddenly the pair stumbled across something extraordinary. A giant flower more than three feet across. Blimey!

Sir Stamford and Dr. Arnold immediately took note of this most unusual specimen sitting on the forest floor. They had found the largest single flower anyone had ever laid eyes on. (Later, the honor was theirs when this species of flower was named after the distinguished duo: *Rafflesia arnoldii*.)

The *Rafflesia* is as strange as it is huge. It has no leaves, roots, or stem. It is in fact an enormous head without a body — a parasite blossom that attaches itself to the vine Tetrastigma. First, blackish buds appear, which swell over nine months to the size of a basketball. When the buds are ready to bloom, each petal suddenly opens. They burst open *so* suddenly that people say you can hear a sucking sound as they slimily unfurl.

But huge and strange isn't enough. It's also smelly. The *Rafflesia* has the nickname "corpse flower" because it stinks to high heaven with the smell of decaying meat. Why? Because it wants to attract flies, of course. It needs the flies for pollination.

The giant flower blooms for only three to five days and then rots, leaving a heap of smelly, decomposing petals. Thank you ever so much, Sir Stamford, but this is just *not* a good Mother's Day present.

500 million miles
(800 million km)

Eta Carinae

One of the biggest stars in our galaxy may not even be there.

The supermassive ball of fire known as Eta Carinae is wildly unstable and ready to blow apart at any moment. In fact, it might *already* have exploded. But we wouldn't know it. We'd just see the star shining as usual. If it blew up today, we wouldn't see the explosion for 7,500 years. (That's how long Eta's light takes to travel to Earth.)

Even if it *hasn't* gone supernova yet, astronomers predict that it will soon. "Soon" to astronomers means within 20,000 years. (Compare that to our sun, which won't end its life for another five billion years.)

Eta Carinae is a monster. Here we see (from a safe distance) how big Eta is next to our sun. It's 500 times the diameter. It's five million times as bright. And it's spinning so fast that it's on the verge of flying apart.

Fortunately for us, Eta is a good 8,000 light-years from Earth. Once, in 1841, it had a giant outburst that briefly made it the second brightest star in the entire sky. The explosion created two enormous lobes called the Homunculus Nebula that are blasting out like twin balloons at 1.5 million miles per hour (2.4 million km/h).

What if our sun was as big as Eta? Well, if the center of Eta was sitting where the sun is, the outer edges of the star would be past the orbit of Jupiter. That wouldn't be so good for us because it would mean the earth was sitting *inside* the star. Which would make things uncomfortably warm.

Wear your sunscreen.

Homunculus Nebula

Orbit of Pluto

Orbit of Jupiter

Eta Carinae

45

How big is a googol?

A googol is a 1 with 100 zeroes after it.

10,000,000,000,000,000,000,000,000,000,000,000,000,000,000,000,000,000,000,000,000,000,000,000,000,000,000,000,0

$$000,000,000,000,000,000,000,000,000,000,000,000$$

or

$$10^{100}$$

Googol

It's bigger than a bazillion. It's bigger than a kajillion. It's bigger than the number of all the known particles in the universe. It's a googol! (And googol is not only bigger, it's better — because it's a *real* number.)

But why even think about a number that's bigger than everything there is?

In 1938, mathematician Edward Kasner knew why. He wanted to show his students that a number could be fantastically large — so big that it would boggle your mind — and still not reach anywhere near infinity. So Dr. Kasner came up with an idea for a really big number — a one with one hundred zeroes after it.

But it needed a name. So he asked his nine-year-old nephew Milton for a suggestion. Milton realized that a number that enormous should have a name that was equally as silly. He came up with the winner — *googol*. And 10^{100} has been called googol ever since.

Let's see if we can imagine how big a googol is. Pretend you're really hungry and you want a googol waffles for breakfast. How high would that stack of waffles be? Can you picture it? *You can't.* A googol waffles would be 10^{80} light-years high. Or, in other words, 10 billion trillion trillion trillion trillion times the size of the universe.

If you counted every proton, neutron, and electron in the entire universe, a googol is 100 quintillion times bigger than that!

By the way, there's an even bigger number than a googol. It's called a googolplex. That's a one with a googol zeroes after it. We won't even go there.

Index

Credits

5 Squid/House: Richard Sands
7 Olympus Mons: NASA/Jet Propulsion Labratory; Mars Globe: NASA
9 Photographic compilation: courtesy Bob Clark, New England Reptile Distributors—N.E.R.D., Plaistow, NH, photograph by Steve Gooch; Train Station: Richard Sands
11 Quetzalcoatlus: Jonathan Blair/Corbis; Fighter Jet: DJ Photography/Dreamstime.com; Sky: Ben Hillman
13 Pyramid: Luke Daniel/iStock Photo; Train: Richard Sand
15 Goliath spider: John Mitchell/Photo Researchers, NY, NY; Table setting: Richard Sands
17 Tokyo: Dreamstime.com; Wave: Rahjahs/Dreamstime.com
19 Basketball game: Sam Forencich/NBAE via GettyImages; Bear: 4dings/Dreamstime.com
21 Girl in the field: Richard Sands; Dragonfly: Ramerwin/Dreamstime.com
23 Chicago: C B 34 Inc./Dreamstime.com; Glacier: Sir Douglass/MorgueFile
25 *Hindenburg*: Corbis; 747: Maarten Wagemans/iStock Photo; Wright Bros. "Flyer": Bettmann/Corbis; Sky: Ben Hillman
27 Asteroid: NASA/JPL/Space Science Institute; New York Skyline: Kevin Connors/MorgueFile
29 Bee hummingbird: Mike Potts/Nature Picture Library, Bristol, England; Elephant bird egg: Colin Keates/DK Limited/Corbis; Bird feet: iStock Photo
31 Buildings: Richard Sands; Sequoia: Mike Norton/Dreamstime.com; Kiwitree/Dreamstime.com
33 Submarine: AP/Wide World Photos; Baseball Stadium: Jason Leathers/iStock Photo, Aflo Images, Japan; Baseball Players: Chris Trotman/Duomo/Corbis; Baseball Players: Chad Neuman/iStock Photo
35 Giraffe: Chrissychristine/Dreamstime.com; Bedroom: Richard Sands
37 Telescope: Photo Courtesy of the NAIC-Arecibo Observatory, a facility of the NSF; Eiffel Tower: Keith Brooks/Dreamstime.com
39 Diamond: Webking/Dreamstime.com; Space Shuttle images: NASA
41 Earth: NASA/Goddard Space Flight Center, Scientific Visualization Studio; Mars: NASA; Canyon: NASA
43 Flower: Compost/Peter Arnold, Inc., Frans Lanting/Minden Pictures; Barn/couple: Ben Hillman
45 Beach/girl: Ben Hillman; Nebula: Jon Morse/University of Colorado/NASA
47 Kid/Waffles: Richard Sands

Special Thanks: Dai Ban, Ethan Ellenberg, Dr. David Hillman, Maizy Hillman, Dr. Manny Hillman, Dwayne Howard, Kate Lampro, Paula Manzanero, Cooper Ronan, Amy Rudnick, Jim Spieler, Robert Taylor, Lindsay Turner.